"I will not allow anyone to walk through my mind with their dirty feet."

Mahatma Gandhi

TIGER SPIRIT WITHIN

"Be equally concern in who you choose to pursue, to who you do not."

Colleen C. Carson

TIGER SPIRIT WITHIN

Teach Acceptance
Inspire Love
Gain Confidence
Encourage Knowledge
Reject Discrimination

Stop Hating
Power Integrity
Indorse Uniqueness
Respect Self
Influence Chance
Trust Wisdom

TIGER SPIRIT WITHIN

"Tiger Spirit Within" is a philosophical conversation
between an Elder and a Child that will take you on a
touching journey of written words explaining
who, what, and why of our bullying mindset. It will
enlighten you to begin your own conversation
of inspiration and a chance to recognize wisdom.

Colleen C. Carson

TIGER SPIRIT WITHIN

TIGER SPIRIT WITHIN

Colleen C. Carson

Carson Power Productions
Vancouver, B. C.

Cover Design by Graphic Artist | Shardel
Book Design by Author | Colleen C. Carson
Editor of Back Cover | Dani Kremeniuk
Editor | Catherine Carrington
Author Page Photo | Photographer | Erik Zennstrom
Crystal's Photo | Photographer | Liz Rosa Photography
Copyright ©2020 Colleen C. Carson

ALL RIGHTS RESERVED. Tiger Spirit Within contains material protected under International and Federal Copyright Laws and Treaties

Any unauthorized reprint or use of this material is prohibited. No part of this Book may be reproduced or transmitted in any form or by any means, electronic or mechanical, including photocopying, recording, or by any information storage and retrieval system without express written/written permission from the author/publisher.

Colleen C. Carson

Others cheered the bullies impart
Amid my fracturing heart
For every taunt, a fracture began
In tears of shamed and terror I ran

The bully continued its predation
Until my heart shattered into isolation
My death would be another's sins
I yearn to be given angel wings

My Mom would sob an 'if only' cry
My Dad would cry a painful 'why'
I cannot cause misery to ones I love
And end a future they speak of

Wisdom of my tiger spirit within
Chance my courage to begin
I must trust I can achieve
The unfolding that I love me

Colleen C. Carson

TIGER SPIRIT WITHIN

"Fight for the things that you care about but do it in a way that will lead others to join you."

Ruth Bader Ginsburg

TIGER SPIRIT WITHIN

DISCOVER

YOUR

TIGER SPIRIT WITHIN

TIGER SPIRIT WITHIN

TIGER SPIRIT WITHIN

Significance of the Tiger Spirit

Tiger Spirit has great resolution, power, courage, and personal strength.
The Tiger Spirit is known as the King of all Beasts.
The Chinese character " 王 " means "the King"
This symbol is exhibited on the Tiger's forehead and signifies bravery and power.
The Tiger Spirit brings purpose, individuality, dedication, and motivation.
Tiger skin in Tantric Buddhism represents the transformation of anger into wisdom and insight, but another belief is to defend the messenger from unknown abuse.

The Tiger Spirit is the leader of its unique realm.
Their power is enchanted by the secrecy and mystical evening sky. The Tiger Spirit senses the power of the moon and urges to introduce the beginnings of aspirations within our hearts.
The Tiger Spirit provides you the power of guided vision, the strength, and self-discipline to disable the combats in your life.

TIGER SPIRIT WITHIN

She dwells in her solace of the night
An influence of the evening twilight
She a vision of soulful reflection
Of inner thought and affection

She in silence inspires all seasons
With wisdom of reflective reasons
She an aura of infinite love
The twilight glow in the sky above

Colleen C. Carson

TIGER SPIRIT WITHIN

"At least 1 in 3 adolescent students in Canada have reported being bullied recently."

Bullying Canada

TIGER SPIRIT WITHIN

"Every 7 minutes a child is bullied."

National Voices for Equality, Education, and Equality

TIGER SPIRIT WITHIN

"Every 30 minutes a child attempts suicide due to bullying."

National Institutes of Health, SAFE, Tony Bartoli

"34 percent of the students have experienced cyber-bullying in their lifetimes."

Cyberbullying Research Center

TIGER SPIRIT WITHIN

"Gay, lesbian, and bisexual youth are 4 times more likely to attempt suicide than their heterosexual counterparts."

Mental Health America

"At least a third of workers are victims of abuse by workplace bullies."

Workplace Bullying Institute

TIGER SPIRIT WITHIN

"Approximately 58 per cent of workplace bullies are women and their primary target are other women."

Workplace Bullying Institute

TIGER SPIRIT WITHIN

"Our children see our nation's leaders bullying others, the fear is they will grow up thinking this is acceptable behavior."

Very Well Family

"Only 20 to 30% of students who are bullied notify adults about the bullying."

Bullying Canada

TIGER SPIRIT WITHIN

"Bullying does not have an age limit we all will be victimized at some point in our lives."

Colleen C. Carson

"A bully represents cowardice in the absence of bravery."

Colleen C. Carson

"The definition of a Bully; A person who habitually seeks to arm or intimidate those whom they perceive as vulnerable."

Oxford Dictionary

"Real change, enduring change, happens one step at a time."

Ruth Bader Ginsburg

The bully imprisons their prey
With fear and cruelty at play
It is not you who is to blame
It is our silence we must shame

Believe in you and say "I rise"
Wipe those tears from your eyes
Do not allow yourself fall victim
Wake your tiger spirit within

                        Colleen C. Carson

"To know courage is to have faith in yourself, hope in others, and love for another."

Colleen C. Carson

What is bullying?

There is no legal definition of bullying, (imagine after decades, even centuries there is still no legal definition at least not in my research).

The Canadian government quotes the following; "Bullying includes actions such as making threats, spreading rumours, attacking someone physically or verbally, and excluding someone from a group on purpose."

Bullying is abusive whether physical, verbal or cyber and when we talk about our children's schoolyard lets make sure we include the corporate and global schoolyards of said grownups. Yes, even I or you have possibly been a bully, asked yourself the following question;

"Have I ever gossip about someone?"

What I do know is bullying degrades another which leaves long-lasting psychological damage and might even result in death. I recall when growing up hearing this ridiculous saying; "Sticks and stones may break my bones, but words will never hurt me."

Its origin is unclear, although reported to have appeared in The Christian Recorder in March 1862, a publication of the African Methodist Episcopal Church, where it is presented as an "old adage" in this form. Through further research, this saying was a literary children's saying. As a child, these words never made sense to me.

The trouble with bullying is for decades, maybe since time began it has been thought of as a rite of passage. Friedrich Nietzsche, the German philosopher, famously said: "That which does not kill us makes us stronger." I do appreciate this quote because I have experienced those very words. But over the years I have heard others recite those words to someone who has been or is being bullied. How does being degraded make one stronger? What is terrifying is bullying is causing death among our youth even the adult populace.

The objective of bullying is attacking the very spirit of heart, and soul to the point of death whether psychological or physical. How terrifying; yet we see it most days and call it something else in order not to disturb the movement of our lifestyle.

Although change has been slight at least there is a movement involving corporations, non-profits, and youth, which gives me hope for abolishment one day. Unfortunately, my scepticism tells me as human beings we become complacent to our ideals when results aren't immediate, or another draws our interest. I have seen this over and over again, and yes, I have had moments of complacency as well because it seemed more comfortable at the time.

"Shame on us!"

The experience of bullying troubled me as a child, but even more so as a mother of children who had been bullied. I have at times lack the bravery to come forward in the protection of the vulnerable while angering in my cowardliness.

I have changed that position, it no longer exists, call it wisdom or a deciding moment from a famous quote by Eldridge Cleaver; "There is no more neutrality in the world. You either have to be part of the solution, or you're going to be part of the problem." I have chosen to be part of the solution.

"Someone once asked me, "Will bullying be stopped?" I answered, "I don't know! I believe children are born with loving, courageous hearts, not hearts of hate; bullying is a taught behaviour. If we the adults exhibit non-bullying behaviour, support our children in their chance to make changes, while using our wisdom of knowledge; I believe we will put an end to our bully mindset."

"Tiger Spirit Within is dedicated to my courageous daughter, Crystal, who was bullied in her childhood, as a teenager, and on occasion her adulthood."

"We delight in the beauty of the butterfly, but rarely admit the changes it has gone through to achieve that beauty."

Maya Angelou

"What we regard as a weakness can in fact be an fundamental power."

Colleen C. Carson

"I will not apologize for my knowledge nor succumb to your ignorance."

Colleen C. Carson

TIGER SPIRIT WITHIN

I asked Colleen, "There have been many books written about bullying, why did you decide to write another? Colleen reply, "I don't know, I sometimes wonder myself, but this I do know we must change our bullying mindset and if that takes the 'Tiger Spirit Within' and thousands of books before or after to make bullying extinct; then read on!"

She continued, "There's a favourite quote that has held dear to my heart and part of my motivation in completing this book." I asked her, "What's the quote?" She responded, "If you want to change the world, pick up your pen and write." I asked, "Who authored the quote?" Colleen replied with a smile, 'Martin Luther King.' She continued, "I believe we have all played a part in the creation and continuance of this intimidating behaviour through complacency or self-actions. In my experience as long as one can blame another the opportunity for change is prolonged."

Colleen continues, "In the beginning, I began with a single blank page and believed my words had ended there, yet the words kept coming and the anxiousness to continue was overwhelming. Over time a page became pages, I knew I had to complete this journey of written words." I asked, "Isn't that what all authors go through when writing a book, no matter the topic?" Colleen countered, "Yes, with one single difference; these written words are not meant to inform, they are meant to reform." We continued to walk in silence of our thoughts.

Colleen resumed, "When I started writing I thought I was writing a child's book on bullying only to come to the end of this journey of words to realize it is meant for all ages." I asked, "Why the change?" She responded, "I realized children will continue to exhibit this bullying behaviour as long as their adult mentors continue accomplishing their inherited bullying mindset."

I asked, "Were you bullied in school?" "Yes," she replied, "I am a dreamer, and I do not apologize for being such. I remember when certain educators and peers would laugh and call me a daydreamer, they made it seem a weakness while being a topic of their humour."

Colleen continued, "It was difficult to be treated with such bias, although it never stopped me from being a dreamer. In fact, my being a dreamer encouraged the commitment of being a forever student which in turn, provided me with a direction in my journey while influencing and aiding my dreams coming true. Dreams are about courage, vision, and to live in the chance of wisdom to know the who, what, and why of others and myself." She pauses and resumes, "Ruth Bader Ginsburg once quoted, "Reading is the key that opens doors to many good things in life."

We continued walking and listening to the gentle movement of the ocean as Colleen spoke, "I'm also a believer. I believe that one day our tiger spirits within will roar into the masses, giving strength in the obliteration of this hideous disease we call bullying." Silence reigned once again; you know the kind of silence that is awkward, yet I knew there was more to come, Colleen had not finished.

After several minutes of walking, she spoke, "At the beginning of hopeful change comes our inspired youth in partnership with knowledgeable adults in opposing the ignorant while achieving awareness of knowledge. You see, you need both the children and elders because many of the bullies of yesterday are still the bullies of today, only older with given power. Some are addressed by titles of leadership who are void of compassion and absence of love for humankind. These bullies conduct their legacy of ignorance triggering fear in our now and future generations. We need the virtue of chance and knowledge of wisdom to identify and change our bullying mindset."

Who is Colleen C. Carson? Well, she was born and raised in Vancouver, Canada in a middle-class family and she is one of five girls. At the age of 18, Colleen began her travels internationally hoping one day to call herself a world traveler, although she laughs about that now, she has travelled and lived abroad. A mother of two; daughter and son, married for 34 years, currently divorced and resides in Vancouver.

Colleen is a woman of substance, determination, and wisdom. She believes our world has been ruled by generations of takers soon to lose their power to the givers, creating the reality of acceptance and respect of all and beyond. Colleen also believes education is the most potent weapon to prevent ignorance.

While walking I told her, "I too have a favourite quote, would you like to hear it?" "Of course!" Colleen replied. "It's a Mahatma Gandhi quote; 'Be the change that you wish to see in the world'." We stopped walking, she looked at me and asked, "What do you think your change would look like?"

I responded, "To be capable of seeing the beauty in me and each of us with respect and accreditation." Colleen smiled and extended an affectionate hug and said, "How lovely that sounds, thank you for your beautiful words." We continued in conversation, as she spoke of her travels, whether a small town or a metropolitan city, business or personal she at times had observed a bullied victim's pain. She did not hesitate to confront bullies about the scars they caused and left behind.

Her worst memories were when her two children experienced bullying. Colleen expressed in a sad tone; "Your child being bullied is every parent's heartbreak. That is why I as a parent and a person must be part of the solution, not part of the problem."

Once again, I asked Colleen, "Do you believe your book will create change?" As she stood there looking out at the ocean, she picked up a stone from the sand, turned to me and with a reassuring voice replied, "Mother Teresa said, "I alone cannot change the world, but I can cast a stone across the waters to create many ripples."

Colleen turned and propelled her stone into the ocean and then turned back to me and with a gentle smile replied, "I look forward to the ripples."

"Blame resides within the origin of Shame."

Colleen C. Carson

TIGER SPIRIT WITHIN

"To my readers, there is no Table of Contents simply because I felt it unnecessary."

Colleen C. Carson

Harmony & Beauty

//

Child: Hello.

Elder: Good day.

Child: May I sit here?

Elder: Yes.

Child: Are you waiting for someone?

Elder: No.

Child: Why do you come here?

Elder: My journey leads me here.

Child: Leads you here?

Elder: Yes.

Child: Why?

Elder: Purpose.

Child: What is your purpose?

Elder: Not what who?

Child: Who then?

Elder: Others.

Child: Are you always alone?

Elder: No.

Child: Why are you alone today?

Elder: I am not.

Child: I do not understand?

Elder: I am with my thoughts.

Child: Your thoughts?

Elder: Yes.

Child: Why your thoughts?

Elder: Reason and clarity.

Child: What are your thoughts?

Elder: Disappointment.

Child: What are you disappointed about?

Elder: Not what, who.

Child: Who has disappointed you?

Elder: Others.

Child: Others, why?

Elder: Difference.

Child: What do you mean difference?

Elder: Not what, who.

Child: Then who?

Elder: Others who do not accept the difference of another.

Child: Why would that disappoint you?

Elder: One's untruth creates another's sadness.

Child: In what way?

Elder: When you speak your ignorance to the ignorant it will incite fear causing the isolation of another.

Child: Why?

Elder: Ignorance.

Child: What is ignorance?

Elder: Lack of knowledge.

Child: Maybe it would be better if we all were the same?

Elder: No.

Child: Why not?

Elder: There would be no reason for knowledge.

Child: No reason?

Elder: If all were the same in appearance and thought, knowledge would be pointless.

Child: You mean we learn through difference?

Elder: Yes.

Child: What is the problem?

Elder: Not what, who.

Child: Then who is the problem?

Elder: Others who permit discrimination to exist and another who accepts their reasoning.

Child: What does discrimination mean?

Elder: The unjust treatment towards one from another based-on difference.

Child: So, your saying difference causes discrimination?

Elder: No.

Child: What do you mean?

Elder: Difference does not cause discrimination; humankind's ignorance causes discrimination.

Child: But why?

Elder: Fear.

Child: Fear of what?

Elder: Not what, who.

Child: Who?

Elder: Others of difference.

Child: Why would someone think that way?

Elder: Once again, ignorance.

Child: What is ignorance?

Elder: I have answered this question, please listen my child. The answer to your question is lack of knowledge.

Child: Okay, then lack of knowledge causes ignorance?

Elder: Yes.

Child: Can you see ignorance?

Elder: Not always.

Child: Why?

Elder: Ignorance sometimes gives the deception of knowledge to conceal hostility.

Child: Why hostility?

Elder: Fear can create hostility.

Child: What makes them do this?

Elder: It does not matter what only why.

Child: What is hostility?

Elder: Someone who is unfriendly and aggressive to others due to difference.

Child: Can hostility cause bullying?

Elder: Bullying is a hostile action.

Child: I was bullied?

Elder: I know.

Child: How do you know?

Elder: Most have.

Child: I felt like I was the only one being bullied?

Elder: Yes, most do.

Child: Were you bullied?

Elder: Yes.

Child: How did you feel?

Elder: Sad.

Child: I felt scared.

Elder: I felt sad for others.

Child: For others, why?

Elder: They only do what they do out of fear.

Child: So, others bully because they fear difference?

Elder: Yes, remember difference comes in many forms.

Child: Then, difference causes bullying?

Elder: No.

Child: I am confused?

Elder: Difference does not cause bullying. It is the ignorant whose fear of difference causes bullying.

Child: What are the differences?

Elder: There are many, you will learn about them in time.

Child: I was also terribly angry at the ones who bullied me, were you?

Elder: No child.

Child: Why?

Elder: I believed in myself not in their fear.

Child: Their words were so mean?

Elder: Yes.

Child: Why did they say such mean words?

Elder: Because words have power.

Child: All words?

Elder: Yes.

Child: Can you explain what you mean?

Elder: It is not about what; it is about who and why.

Child: Okay, who and why?

Elder: Humankind's cruel words are always spoken to benefit oneself.

Child: How?

Elder: A reaction.

Child: A reaction?

Elder: Yes. Their goal is to seek a negative reaction of another to sense their inner power.

Child: Can I stop their words from making me feel sad and scared?

Elder: Yes. Replace the cruel words with kind words.

Child: Why?

Elder: Words should achieve a positive reaction. If words do not than what is the purpose of the one who speaks cruel words?

Child: I guess to hurt my feelings?

Elder: Yes.

Child: Why do I remember the mean words more than kind words?

Elder: Cruel words are echo longer than the kind words because the listener, like you my child, lacks self-worth.

Child: I still do not understand?

Elder: Cruel words are recited in fear to create fear, kind words in confidence to create confidence. Humankind seems destine to give power to the cruel words rather than that of kind words.

Child: Why?

Elder: Self-worth.

Child: Does that mean the one who bullies is also in fear?

Elder: Yes.

Child: Why?

Elder: Because they too have been bullied while living in the ignorance of their fear.

Child: Really, and that is why?

Elder: The appearance of being better and having power over another gives the bully a sense of worth, although a false sense nevertheless it lessens their fear.

Child: But you said people who do these things have no worth?

Elder: No, I did not say that, all humankind has worth of purpose. The ignorant through fear suffers the absence of self-worth.

Child: What is self-worth?

Elder: Having faith in yourself.

Child: Self-worth is having faith in me?

Elder: Yes, the belief and respect of one's purpose; self-worth.

Child: Is self-worth hard to achieve?

Elder: That is up to you my child.

Child: Wouldn't you feel hurt from mean words?

Elder: No. I would rather give power to knowledge than to ignorance.

Child: Did you cry when you were bullied?

Elder: My child, you have tears in your eyes?

Child: Yes, I am sad that someone wants to be mean to me.

Elder: Your tears are important and should not be wasted on another's ignorance. Why do you allow that?

Child: Are you saying it is wrong to cry?

Elder: No, crying is important, but your tears should be worthy of yourself and others. In whom you cry for, are they worthy of your tears?

Child: I do not think so, but I cannot help it, being bullied was very frightening to me and they really hurt my feelings.

Elder: Yes, I understand your pain and it saddens me that you still live in the custody of their words and actions.

Child: How would you change that if you were me?

Elder: My child, I am not you.

Child: Okay, but how would you stop crying?

Elder: I would cry for my sadness, but not for the ignorance of others.

Child: How is that different from my crying?

Elder: You cry the memory instead of the moment.

Child: How is that different?

Elder: When you cry in the moment your tears our yours to heal, and a new lesson to be learned. When you cry in the memory you prevent yourself from healing and the lesson is delayed.

Child: Okay, tell me what to do?

Elder: You begin by having faith in you and knowing your worth to yourself and others.

Child: Are not tears about your own sadness?

Elder: Tears do not always mean sadness. Tears were given to humankind for many reasons. Tears improve your vision of the world you see, tears are guided in your passion of love, life, and loss. Tears bring the solemn of rest when the wake is plentiful. Your tears are equally meant to share among you and others.

Child: So, crying is necessary?

Elder: Yes.

Child: I cried when I was bullied because I felt so alone?

Elder: No one's alone my child.

Child: No one?

Elder: No one.

Child: Why do I sometimes feel like I am?

Elder: You must discover trust.

Child: What do you mean trust?

Elder: Not what, who.

Child: Then who?

Elder: Trust in yourself and others.

Child: Why trust?

Elder: Without trust, love is not shared.

Child: Do you think another loves me?

Elder: It does not matter what I think, it matters what you think.

Child: I believe I am loved.

Elder: Yes, we are all loved.

Child: You mean by our family and friends?

Elder: Yes, and others.

Child: Why was I ashamed to talk about being bullied?

Elder: Imperfection.

Child: I do not understand?

Elder: You and others want to be perfect.

Child: I want to be perfect like others?

Elder: Yes.

Child: What is so wrong with wanting to be perfect?

Elder: Perfection does not exist my child.

Child: Perfection does not exist, but I have seen it?

Elder: No, you just want to believe you have.

Child: You mean no one or nothing is perfect?

Elder: Well. One exception.

Child: Only one?

Elder: Yes.

Child: What is the exception?

Elder: Your soul.

Child: My soul?

Elder: Yes, my child.

Child: Why are our souls perfect?

Elder: Purity.

Child: What does that mean?

Elder: Only knows truth.

Child: Truth?

Elder: Yes.

Child: So, does not tell lies?

Elder: I did not say that.

Child: You did not?

Elder: I told you your soul knows truth.

Child: If knowing the truth, you must also speak the truth?

Elder: Your soul has no spoken words.

Child: I do not understand?

Elder: Your soul does not speak as you do because of its purpose.

Child: Purpose?

Elder: Yes. Your soul's purpose is to inspire your truth of existence.

Child: I am not sure if I understand?

Elder: You will learn in time.

Child: So, no one's perfect?

Elder: No one.

Child: And that is okay?

Elder: Yes.

Child: Is seeing others as perfect wrong?

Elder: No. It is unforgiving.

Child: Unforgiving?

Elder: Yes.

Child: Why?

Elder: When you see others as perfect you're unforgiving of your imperfections.

Child: How do I stop myself?

Elder: Confidence.

Child: How do I become confident?

Elder: Knowledge.

Child: Knowledge?

Elder: Yes, the more you know, the more confident you become.

Child: What is the most important part of knowledge?

Elder: Diversity.

Child: Diversity?

Elder: Yes.

Child: What does that mean?

Elder: Knowledge of all humankind, yourself included, and of course the world you live in.

Child: Why?

Elder: Understanding how others are unique also allows you to acknowledge your uniqueness.

Child: What do you mean?

Elder: Not what, who.

Child: Okay, who?

Elder: Each human is unique creating diversity.

Child: Why do we need diversity?

Elder: Beauty and harmony.

Child: Beauty and harmony of what?

Elder: Not what, who.

Child: Then who?

Elder: You and others.

Child: I don't understand?

Elder: The world is a wondrous creation of the beauty of uniqueness. By accepting another's uniqueness with respect will bring harmony in the co-existence of humankind.

Child: I still don't understand?

Elder: Look around you; what do you see?

Child: I see a forest.

Elder: Yes, anything else?

Child: Nope, just the forest. What do you see?

Elder: I see diversity.

Child: What diversity?

Elder: Not what, who.

Child: Why do you need diversity in a forest?

Elder: Without diversity, the forest would not exist.

Child: Please explain?

Elder: I asked you, what do you see, and you replied a forest.

Child: Yes I did, was that wrong?

Elder: No, there is no wrong or right to your answer.

Child: How do you mean?

Elder: You saw only of the forest not its diversity.

Child: Then what do you see?

Elder: Not what, who.

Child: Okay, who?

Elder: I see each as unique within the forest. I see trees; tall, short, big, and small. I see plants, soil, grass, flowers, rocks, streams, paths, creatures, insects; many and all unique in their existence. I can smell each tree's scent in the air as I breathe. I'm surrounded by diverse colours of brilliance which enlighten me. I bear witness to the beauty of diversity and the harmony of equal respect inspired by all in this forest to co-exist in relevance.

Child: You see all that?

Elder: Yes.

Child: How?

Elder: Knowledge.

Child: Knowledge of the forest?

Elder: Yes, just like with you in your community.

Child: My community? Where I live?

Elder: Yes.

Child: What do you know about my community?

Elder: Not what, who.

Child: Then who?

Elder: Your community is like the forest, its origin is about diversity. The difference in your community to the forest is the forest has an acceptance and respect for each and all uniqueness in order to co-exist in growth.

Child: The forest knows that?

Elder: Yes, you seem to be surprised.

Child: Well, without us there wouldn't be a forest, right?

Elder: No, without the forest there would be no humankind.

Child: Why?

Elder: Survival is communal with all who are living in this world.

Child: Is that how the forest survives?

Elder: The forest exists in the reliance shared among all and the equal respect of uniqueness.

Child: What is the difference between the forest and my community?

Elder: Acceptance.

Child: Do you think my community has diversity?

Elder: Your question is not for me to answer, the answer is yours to speak.

Child: I think it does?

Elder: Many communities would rather live in ignorance motivated by fear rather than knowledge motivated by confidence in accepting the uniqueness and equality of humankind.

Child: If my community is like that, am I as well?

Elder: Only you can answer your question.

Child: I don't think I am, do you?

Elder: You seek knowledge.

Child: How does knowledge change ignorance and fear?

Elder: Once again, knowledge gains confidence and lessen's one's fear. Knowledge is about the uniqueness of oneself, chance of exploration, and wisdom of encouragement in learning about you and others.

Child: So, ignorance is about fear; knowledge is about confidence?

Elder: Yes.

Child: I think ignorance can be very hurtful.

Elder: Yes.

Child: I would rather be knowledgeable and happy then ignorant and scared.

Elder: Well-chosen.

Child: You say the forest respects each for their uniqueness and yet humankind doesn't.

Elder: Yes.

Child: But isn't humankind the most powerful of all else that exists in our world?

Elder: All are equal in power and purpose in the diversity of your world.

Child: I don't think we're doing that.

Elder: No, unfortunately.

Child: So everyone and everything should be accepted equally?

Elder: Yes, all in your world are equal to co-exist.

Child: Why?

Elder: Importance of purpose in the confidence of beauty and harmony in the world you live.

Child: I don't know if we are capable?

Elder: It's simply about knowledge and choice.

Child: Is that what's causing your disappointment?

Elder: Yes.

Child: Do you think you will stop being disappointed?

Elder: I'm hopeful.

Child: Is humankind just selfish?

Elder: No.

Child: How can we change the way humankind is?

Elder: Begin with you, if you truly believe, others will follow.

Child: Why didn't I see what you saw in the forest?

Elder: You must learn the who of you, the what of belief, and the why of purpose to achieve the knowledge of acceptance to co-exist in harmony and beauty.

Child: I think I'm beginning to understand.

Elder: Yes, I believe you are.

"Fear creates disappointment.
Courage creates achievement."

Colleen C. Carson

Unique You

TIGER SPIRIT WITHIN

Child: You told me I'm unique?

Elder: Yes, I did.

Child: How am I unique?

Elder: There is no other like you.

Child: How does that make me unique?

Elder: No one is the same.

Child: Then everyone is unique?

Elder: Yes.

Child: What makes all of us unique?

Elder: Your gifts.

Child: What gifts?

Elder: The gifts given at birth.

Child: I was given gifts at birth?

Elder: Yes.

Child: What are these gifts?

Elder: That is for you to discover.

Child: Do you know my gifts?

Elder: Perhaps.

Child: Can you tell me what my gifts are?

Elder: No.

Child: If you know why won't you tell me?

Elder: You must learn for yourself my child.

Child: Why?

Elder: When humankind give and receive gifts each gains something. The giver a sense of fulfilment and the receiver a sense of worth; both feelings inspired each.

Child: Okay, I still don't understand why you can't tell me?

Elder: By learning of your gifts you will experience an appreciation of fulfilment, worth, and inspiration.

Child: When will I learn of these gifts?

Elder: That's up to you.

Child: What do you mean?

Elder: Learning is your decision.

Child: How long does it normally take?

Elder: A lifetime for some; moments for others.

Child: Wow, a lifetime is a long time, how come?

Elder: The question is for you to answer.

Child: Is the answer about learning?

Elder: Yes.

Child: Okay, now I'm really confused?

Elder: Why?

Child: Some take a lifetime, but others take moments, how can you learn your gifts in moments?

Elder: Why do you ask?

Child: To understand?

Elder: For some; moments is a lifetime.

Child: Are we talking about living?

Elder: I believe so.

Child: How does a baby whose just been born know how to learn?

Elder: Learning comes at first breath.

Child: Please explain?

Elder: To breathe is to learn, to learn is to live, to live is to achieve your purpose.

Child: I'm confused.

Elder: That will change.

Child: Does that mean I've been learning since I was born?

Elder: Yes.

Child: This seems so complicated?

Elder: No. I will explain in time.

Child: Being unique is good?

Elder: Yes.

Child: My gifts make me unique?

Elder: Yes.

Child: Do you have gifts like me?

Elder: Not like you, but yes.

Child: I think I know one of your gifts?

Elder: Yes.

Child: I believe it's kindness.

Elder: Thank you, but that's not a gift.

Child: Then what would it be?

Elder: Your tiger spirit within.

Child: What spirit?

Elder: Your tiger spirit.

Child: I have a tiger in me?

Elder: Yes, the power of your tiger spirit is within you.

Child: What is this power?

Elder: Power of belief.

Child: Belief in what?

Elder: Not what, who.

Child: Belief in others?

Elder: And you.

Child: I have birth gifts and now my tiger spirit within?

Elder: Yes.

Child: Are they different or the same?

Elder: They are different.

Child: How are they different?

Elder: Birth gifts are given, your tiger spirit within is a choice.

Child: What are birth gifts?

Elder: Birth gifts are your talents.

Child: Give me an example of a talent?

Elder: A talent could be working with your hands like a carpenter, a beautiful voice like of a singer, and so on. Talents create your purpose.

Child: What is purpose?

Elder: A purpose is the role you create in the performance of your existence.

Child: Meaning?

Elder: Your uniqueness of self.

Child: How many gifts was I given at birth?

Elder: That is for you to find out.

Child: How do I know my gifts?

Elder: Knowledge will ignite your gift or gifts of purpose.

Child: What will I do with this gift or gifts?

Elder: Once again, that decision is yours.

Child: Why are we given these gifts?

Elder: To create a community of beauty and harmony; a purpose.

Child: Do we all have a purpose?

Elder: Yes.

Child: Our gifts give us a purpose?

Elder: Yes.

Child: How do my gifts create a community of beauty and harmony?

Elder: Your gifts can bring happiness to the sad, light to the darkness, speech to the silent, liberty to the suppressed, warmth to the cold, remedy to the sick, possibility to the disable, inspiration to the wearisome, and love to the lonely.

Child: Couldn't your gifts also bring bad to others?

Elder: No, gifts are not evil. Evil is only created through humankind's hunger for power and control.

Child: I want my gifts to make others happy.

Elder: As well as yourself.

Child: Can anyone stop me from learning my gifts?

Elder: Yes, why do you ask?

Child: I don't know why I asked, but who can?

Elder: You.

Child: I could stop myself?

Elder: Yes.

Child: But why would I do that?

Elder: Fear and ignorance

Child: So would I stop myself out of fear and ignorance?

Elder: Yes, I believe I have explained; they both live in partnership.

Child: How can I stop my fear?

Elder: Your tiger spirit within you.

Child: I will then have no fear?

Elder: The choice is yours to determine.

Child: I don't understand?

Elder: Humankind seems to have accepted fear rather than not. They teach their children of fear as soon as their children understand spoken words.

Child: But why?

Elder: Because of their fear.

Child: My parents love me and want no harm to come to me, is that wrong?

Elder: Love is not wrong, and we are here to protect each other which is part of life survival. I have yet to speak of that, I speak of fear.

Child: Then what do you mean?

Elder: There are others who have unused gifts due to ignorance and fear. At the end of their existence, they will be asked only three questions and their answers will either bring a sense joy or regret.

Child: What are those three questions?

Elder: Did you love yourself equal to others? Did you learn as a student equally as a teacher? Did you live your purpose?

Child: I don't want to have any regrets when I'm old.

Elder: This has nothing to do with age.

Child: I thought that's what you meant?

Elder: No. This will come at the end of your life existence.

Child: Help me not to have regrets at the end of my existence?

Elder: Only you my child can determine how you live.

Child: You told me the questions, please tell me the answers?

Elder: The answers will be yours to speak. I can't give you the answers to your choices. What I can express to you is the difference between joy and regret.

Child: Okay, what's the difference?

Elder: I can or I could, I will or I would, I shall or I should. There is a choice by what method you will love, learn, and live your life.

Child: Could you explain what you just said?

Elder: In the confidence of knowledge you will express the words; I can, I will, and I shall. In ignorance you will express the words; I could, I would, and I should. You will limit the knowing of your gifts and purpose if you live in fear and ignorance.

Child: I feel this urgency?

Elder: Be patient my child. Remember, each moment you are, you are meant to be.

Child: What does that mean?

Elder: Be present in your now for that is your only moment of life.

Child: Do you mean I'm going to die?

Elder: Death comes to all when your purpose is fulfilled.

Child: Oh, I get that, I just thought you knew something I didn't.

Elder: You have time my child.

Child: What are other things I will learn?

Elder: Self-compassion.

Child: What is self-compassion?

Elder: Being kind to yourself when experiencing life suffering.

Child: How do you mean life suffering?

Elder: Life is a sequence of disappointments and achievements. Humankind has other names in replace of mine known as failures and successes or winning and losing.

Child: I don't want to fail?

Elder: Then, you will not learn.

Child: Are you telling me that I must fail in order to learn?

Elder: Yes.

Child: That doesn't make sense to me, why?

Elder: Disappointment is where you will learn wisdom to chance the bliss of achievement.

Child: Does that mean I learn nothing from success?

Elder: No.

Child: Then what do I learn from success?

Elder: Achievement teaches confidence while in the bliss of triumph, achievement of purpose, and hope.

Child: What do I learn from failure?

Elder: Disappointment teaches you a lesson, eliminates complacency, builds creativity, and of course assists you overcoming fear.

Child: My uncle told me only the successful are famous?

Elder: Is being famous important to you?

Child: Yes, I think so.

Elder: Why do you think fame is about achievement?

Child: Isn't it?

Elder: Fame can be the best of you or the worst of you. It might be given not earned which means fame might have nothing to do with achievement or as you call it; success.

Child: You make fame seem like a terrible thing.

Elder: Sometimes it might leave you in more pain than happiness.

Child: I still don't want to fail?

Elder: Of course you don't. If you don't accept disappointment as a lesson to learn, then your life will be that of settling.

Child: What does that mean?

Elder: It means my child; you will simply exist not knowing your purpose.

Child: Why?

Elder: Fearing your next step will keep you crawling through life no longer believing in your purpose of achievement and your existence will flourish in regret.

Child: Is failing that important?

Elder: Yes, both disappointment and achievement are equally important. Disappointment will define you in courage, and achievement will define you in purpose .

Child: Does that mean in order to succeed I've got to make myself fail?

Elder: No my child. You must listen. Allowing yourself the opportunity to the want of achievement allows you the chance of disappointment. If you have learnt the wisdom of your past, your achievements will become greater than your disappointments. Failure will only happen if the necessity of learning prevails.

Child: This is not going to be easy is it?

Elder: Remember this, for every disappointment, a lesson is learned, and a rainbow is earned. Achievement is only earned not given.

Child: You make failing sound like a good thing?

Elder: If you are absent of disappointment, you are also absent of the chance to achieve. In order to value achievement you must experience disappointment.

Child: Why do you say disappointment instead of failure?

Elder: Humankind accepts disappointment easier than they do failure, although both mean the same; the reaction is different.

Child: In what way?

Elder: Failure is unacceptable, yet disappointment is expected.

Child: What about achievement instead of success?

Elder: Humankind seems to gain more in achieving than they do with success.

Child: So, disappointment is just part of learning?

Elder: Yes. Your chance in knowing the wisdom of purpose.

Child: That's the only way I'm going to discover my gifts?

Elder: Yes.

Child: You said I must be kind to myself, why not others?

Elder: Self-compassion is about you and compassion is about others.

Child: What is compassion?

Elder: Compassion is being kind to others.

Child: So self-compassion is like compassion?

Elder: Yes, they both relate to kindness. Self-compassion is a kindness towards yourself, whereas compassion is a kindness toward others.

Child: If I have self-compassion, then I must have compassion?

Elder: Not necessarily.

Child: Why?

Elder: Some have kindness for others yet not for themselves as alike you have kindness for yourself yet not for others. This is not frequent but it does exist.

Child: You can have both?

Elder: Yes.

Child: What does self-compassion have to do with confidence?

Elder: Confidence enhances self-compassion.

Child: What about compassion?

Elder: Compassion gives kindness to others for them to know they are not alone in their life's moments particularly if they're sensing disappointment.

Child: I just can't see why anyone would want to be disappointed?

Elder: No one wants to be disappointed, my child, its life's way of giving you the prospect of chance and knowing the bliss of achievement ultimately fulfilling your purpose.

Child: How do you feel when you've failed?

Elder: You know the answer to this question.

Child: I just want your view.

Elder: Many different feelings sometimes even loneliness.

Child: I thought you said no one is alone?

Elder: Yes, no one.

Child: Then why loneliness?

Elder: Disappointment causes inner emotions such as shame, sadness, stress, and even depression. Disappointment can sometimes initiate loneliness due to a sense of self.

Child: Sense of self?

Elder: Yes. Ego is a sense of self-importance; a self-conceit of excessive pride in oneself. Because of this, you create a refuge of loneliness to avoid the possibility of others knowing you didn't succeed, rather, you failed.

Child: I think I'm beginning to like your words rather than mine. Like achievement than success and disappointment than failure.

Elder: Yes.

Child: I think I'd feel ashamed of failure, wouldn't you?

Elder: No. I would trust in the others I love and who love me.

Child: Is that what you meant about trust and love?

Elder: Yes, my child.

Child: So, you're not really alone, you just choose to be alone?

Elder: Yes.

Child: Does compassion make you more confident?

Elder: No, it's about kindness.

Child: Is that why I was bullied because I had no self-compassion?

Elder: No, you had the absense of self-worth. Once again, living in perfection gives others power.

Child: Is all this about me or about the one who bullies?

Elder: Both.

Child: Does the bully and bullied experience the same lack of self-worth?

Elder: Yes.

Child: Does that mean if both had self-worth there would not be any bullying?

Elder: Yes. Knowledge creates confidence and self-worth which removes the ignorance and the fear of difference.

Child: I have heard others speak of discrimination?

Elder: Yes?

Child: Is bullying like discrimination?

Elder: Yes, but once again as I said ignorance is the actual cause. You can give whatever title; Racism, Sexism, Classism, Anti-Semitism, and Heterosexism, and so on; they are all fears initiated by ignorance.

Child: Can we stop discrimination?

Elder: Yes, you can.

Child: How?

Elder: Acceptance.

Child: What do you mean acceptance?

Elder: Acceptance by embracing uniqueness.

Child: Will that end bullying?

Elder: The beginning to ending the torment of the bully and bullied.

Child: Do you think we can?

Elder: Yes, humankind is capable, but it is whether they are willing.

Child: Why would anyone not want to see the end of bullying?

Elder: There are those who prefer to live in ignorance rather than knowledge.

Child: Why would anyone want to live in fear? I remember what fear felt like when I was being bullied. I was so scared, lonely, and sad.

Elder: Others that choose ignorance have also accepted fear, believing they exist in the shadows of threat.

Child: I say no to being ignorant?

Elder: Well-chosen.

Child: Do you think I am willing?

Elder: Yes, I believe so, do you think you are willing?

Child: I believe I am. Why do you believe I can?

Elder: Because you are here.

Child: Sometimes I wonder who I am, is that strange?

Elder: No, this wonder is not uncommon.

Child: How do I find my purpose?

Elder: There are many wonders in life's journey in the discovery of purpose. Living your tiger spirit within will create the chance of knowing your gifts of purpose, while accepting the uniqueness of you. Hence, accepting and respecting the who you are, the what in you, and the why of you, you will no longer live within the cruelty of others.

Child: I do not understand?

Elder: Without respect; thoughts are cruel. If you live in their cruelty, then you will not be the why, what, and who of you.

Child: Are you saying I feel like I am strange because of others?

Elder: It does not matter what I think, it matters who you are.

Child: I would really like to know who I am.

Elder: Yes, I believe you.

Child: How do I begin to change?

Elder: You already have.

Child: Is that part of my uniqueness?

Elder: No, it is part of your tiger spirit.

Child: Does everyone have a tiger spirit within them?

Elder: Yes.

Child: Wouldn't that make us all the same?

Elder: No.

Child: I do not understand?

Elder: Your uniqueness are your gifts given; your tiger spirit is by choice. This will allow you to believe in the uniqueness of you and accept the uniqueness of others.

Child: My gifts and my spirit will do that?

Elder: Yes.

Child: I still do not quite understand?

Elder: When your tiger spirit roars, you will lead with courage and follow in truth. Your existence will be known with respect and acceptance by you and others and you will then know your uniqueness of purpose.

Child: I have been told there are those who lead and those who follow?

Elder: There is no truth to your belief. Each will lead as well as follow in the equal equity to learn. What you speak of is humankind's way to control and keep silent your tiger spirit within.

Child: Keep silent my spirit?

Elder: Yes,

Child: How do I change my way of thinking?

Elder: You begin.

Child: Begin with what?

Elder: Not what, who.

Child: Who then?

Elder: You and your tiger spirit within.

Child: Do you believe I can live my tiger spirit within?

Elder: Why do you ask me a question that only you can answer?

Child: I guess I want your approval?

Elder: My approval, although satisfying has little to do with you believing in yourself.

Child: I can do this?

Elder: The choice is yours.

Child: How do I learn about my tiger spirit within me?

Elder: In the presence of your thoughts.

Child: Why there?

Elder: Your tiger spirit lives within your thoughts.

Child: How do I start?

Elder: Ask the who, what, and why of you then continue with how you want and need to arrive within the purpose of being.

Child: And I do this through my thoughts?

Elder: Yes.

Child: Why did I not think I was worth much?

Elder: You know the answer.

Child: Why can you see my uniqueness and I could not?

Elder: You valued others as perfect while lessening your uniqueness of self-worth.

Child: Yes, I wanted to be like others.

Elder: Humankind's ultimate weakness.

Child: I am kind of liking being unique.

Elder: Yes, you have begun.

Child: I think I am beginning to understand.

Elder: Yes, I believe you are.

Best
Of
You

Child: Hello.

Spirit: Hello.

Child: Are you my tiger spirit within?

Spirit: Yes.

Child: You look like a tiger.

Spirit: Is my appearance important?

Child: I guess it makes no difference.

Spirit: You came to speak to me?

Child: Yes.

Spirit: Why?

Child: I just want to know about you.

Spirit: What would you like to know?

Child: Who are you?

Spirit: I am the best of you.

Child: The best of me?

Spirit: Yes.

Child: How do you know that?

Spirit: I am within you.

Child: What do you mean by the best of me?

Spirit: If you live in the reflection of your spirit you will share beauty and harmony within humankind and the world you live in.

Child: Is it difficult to be the best of me?

Spirit: Sometimes, but you must be willing to continue.

Child: If I do, will others accept me?

Spirit: Most will but there will be some that will not.

Child: Why?

Spirit: They will fear who you are.

Child: Why?

Spirit: You will know courage.

Child: And that is why they will not accept me because I have courage?

Spirit: Yes.

Child: Who are they?

Spirit: The ignorant.

Child: Explain?

Spirit: Ignorance has no control over courage which causes them a sense of fear.

Child: That is disappointing.

Spirit: Why is their acceptance important to you?

Child: I do not know.

Spirit: Remember, those who seek courage will seek you; the choice is one's decision to act.

Child: How do I begin to live within my spirit?

Spirit: Love.

Child: Love?

Spirit: Yes, you give complete love.

Child: Complete love?

Spirit: Yes, no limits and no conditions. Some call this love, unconditional.

Child: Is loving unconditionally all I must do?

Spirit: No, there are more. Would you like to know all of them?

Child: Yes, all of them.

Spirit: Very well, but I must remind you that you have not yet achieved all of these, but with the strength of character I believe you will.

Child: I will?

Spirit: Yes.

Child: What are they?

Spirit: First, through love, you will experience acceptance.

Child: Of others?

Spirit: And you.

Child: How?

Spirit: You will begin to teach acceptance.

Child: To who?

Spirit: Whoever you love and encounter.

Child: What will happen?

Spirit: Through your teaching, you will encourage knowledge.

Child: Why?

Spirit: Whether teacher or student, you both learn equally.

Child: I believe in learning.

Spirit: Yes, I know.

Child: Okay, from there what would come next?

Spirit: You must always respect yourself and others.

Child: Myself as well?

Spirit: Yes. Respecting yourself allows others to respect you. Respecting each other brings a sense of confidence.

Child: So, having confidence allows you to respect yourself?

Spirit: Yes.

Child: A sense of confidence is just about respect?

Spirit: No, confidence is knowledge; the more you learn, the more you will strengthen your confidence.

Child: Does this happen to everyone?

Spirit: It is by choice.

Child: I want to.

Spirit: Then seek knowledge, and respect your uniqueness, while indorsing your self-worth, which will grow confidence.

Child: My self-worth is the confidence in my uniqueness?

Spirit: Yes, I believe you understand this part of you.

Child: Yes, I am excited to say I am learning more about myself.

Spirit: Very Good.

Child: What more will I need to do?

Spirit: With love, respect, knowledge, confidence, and the acceptance in the uniqueness of you and others ignorance and fear will lessen.

Child: Then what?

Spirt: You will begin to reject discrimination and the influence of hate.

Child: If I do as you say, will that end bullying?

Spirit: It is a beginning.

Child; Just the beginning?

Spirit: You will need others to assist you to end this pestilence; you and others have created.

Child: I created?

Spirit: All have been a part of this problem, the solution for change will have no excuses. Even then there will be the ignorant that will refuse.

Child: Why?

Spirit: Because there will always be others who prefer living in their ignorance and fear rather than accept difference.

Child: I want to stop bullying forever.

Spirit: Yes.

Child: What do I have to do to do this?

Spirit: Give power to integrity.

Child: What is integrity?

Spirit: Integrity is the honesty and truthfulness of your actions. Integrity is also about honour, the virtue of ethics, morals, and principles.

Child: That is a lot to remember.

Spirit: Begin by remembering to treat others and your world with respect, worth, and equality.

Child: I can do that; then?

Spirit: Influence the chance to awaken your vision of teaching while being the student.

Child: What does that mean?

Spirit: Always be open and welcoming to opportunities where you can learn whether that of the student or teacher.

Child: What opportunities?

Spirit: You will know them when they present themselves.

Child: I feel excited because I believe I can do this.

Spirit: Very good. Now this is important for you to remember; trust wisdom and your truth will be told.

Child: Who will tell it?

Spirit: You.

Child: Will I know joy then?

Spirit: Would you like to?

Child: Yes.

Spirit: I believe you will.

Child: Really?

Spirit: Yes.

Child: How will I begin?

Spirit: Love is where you begin.

Child: Love of others?

Spirit: And you.

Child: How do you love others?

Spirit: You begin with one.

Child: One?

Spirit: Yes.

Child: Who do I begin loving first?

Spirit: You.

Child: I am first, why?

Spirit: To love others you must love yourself.

Child: Wouldn't that make me egotistical?

Spirit: No.

Child: Why?

Spirit: You love yourself equal to others not more than others.

Child: Equal?

Spirit: Yes, equal.

Child: Okay, what about hate?

Spirit: Hate does not exist within love.

Child: Why?

Spirit: Hatred is a fear that only exists in the ignorant.

Child: You talk like someone else I know.

Spirit: Yes.

Child: But what about the others who do not love you or don't even like you?

Spirit: If you live within truth you will not be acquainted with the ignorant.

Child: Do I stay away from them?

Spirit: They will stay away from you because they no longer want nor feel the need to learn.

Child: Being ignorant is sad?

Spirit: Yes, and disturbing because it brings untruth.

Child: Untruth?

Spirit: Yes.

Child: Is untruth like a lie?

Spirit: Similar and at times the same.

Child: What is the difference between a lie and an untruth?

Spirit: A lie is to hide the truth, whereas an untruth avoids the truth.

Child: How can we end untruth?

Spirit: Give power to integrity.

Child: Can you explain integrity just a little more?

Spirit: It is a form of knowing the difference between good and bad, right and wrong, justice and injustice while giving certainty to others.

Child: Do I have confidence?

Spirit: That is not a question I can answer.

Child: Why?

Spirit: You are the answer, to ask means confidence is absent.

Child: What happens when I have confidence?

Spirit: Belief in you.

Child: I really want to end bullying do you think that is my purpose?

Spirit: It does not matter what I think, it matters what you think.

Child: I do not know, but I would like my purpose to end bullying.

Spirit: Would you?

Child: Yes.

Spirit: Why?

Child: I guess because I do not want to live in fear anymore.

Spirit Live the best of you and you will not be bullied.

Child: I just think it is not going to be easy?

Spirit: Nothing worthwhile is easy, but when achieved rewarding.

Child: What will my reward be?

Spirit: Joy.

Child: Joy?

Spirit: Yes.

Child: I will be happy?

Spirit: You will know joy.

Child: I do not understand is not happiness and joy the same?

Spirit: No.

Child: What is the difference?

Spirit: Others create your happiness you create your joy.

Child: So, wouldn't I know both?

Spirit: Yes, you will know the happiness of joy.

Child: I like talking to you.

Spirit: I like talking to you.

Child: You seem very smart.

Spirit: You seem very smart.

Child: You think I am?

Spirit: Yes, don't you?

Child: Sometimes I do and sometimes I do not.

Spirit: When do you not think your smart?

Child: I do not know; it is kind of different times.

Spirit: Can you tell me of a different time?

Child: I do not like who I am when I feel dumb.

Spirit: When do you feel dumb?

Child: When others can do things I cannot, or they know more than me.

Spirit: That does not mean you are dumb.

Child: But that is how I feel.

Spirit: You should appreciate other's talents without envy. Welcome their talents with respect and confidence. You as well as they might know just how smart you are.

Child: Do you really think so?

Spirit: Yes, to help others or have others help you grows confidence through the intention of acceptance.

Child: Do you think I am envious of others?

Spirit: Are you?

Child: Yes, I think so?

Spirit: Do you want to change?

Child: Why do you ask?

Spirit: You must believe in you to accept your imperfections while acknowledging nothing is perfect. Be significant to the uniqueness of you and others while encouraging knowledge.

Child: I guess.

Spirit: Have you thought that they might feel imperfect to you?

Child: I never thought others would feel imperfect because of me.

Spirit: Yes. If I told you that it was not others who made you feel dumb instead it was you; would you be surprised?

Child: That does not make sense.

Spirit: If you had confidence in yourself, then others would too.

Child: Are you saying that is why I was bullied?

Spirit: Why are you seeking to blame yourself?

Child: I must have some sort of blame for being bullied.

Spirit: Blame has no solution.

Child: Well, then what are you telling me?

Spirit: An awareness to learn and accept yourself and others for your uniqueness is the acceptance of imperfection and the knowing that perfection does not exist allowing you the freedom from others cruelty.

Child: I guess?

Spirit: You agree then?

Child: Yes, I guess so.

Spirit: Very Good.

Child: I must stop thinking that imperfection is a weakness.

Spirit: Remember, an imperfection can sometimes be a strength within you.

Child: My friend was the one who told me about you.

Spirit: Yes.

Child: I did not know you existed.

Spirit: It no longer matters.

Child: I need to become you.

Spirit: No, you want to be the best of you.

Child: What is the difference between who, what, and why?

Spirit: Uniqueness of seeking chance and wisdom is the who. Knowledge of teacher and student is in discovering what. Purpose of courage, integrity, faith, hope, and love is the why.

Child: The why of purpose, the who of uniqueness, and the what of knowledge will be the best of me?

Spirit: Yes.

Child: What is the difference between want and need?

Spirit: It is simple; the why of who you want to be to what you need to be.

Child: Please explain?

Spirit: Want is an opportunity and need a necessity. Do you have any further questions?

Child: Yes. I think I know the answer to my question, I would just like your opinion.

Spirit: Yes, what is your question?

Child: Do you think words have power?

Spirit: Yes, words have immense power.

Child: Why?

Spirit: Words can break a heart or mend it, bring tears or laughter, strengthen or weaken, elate or dishearten; words matter.

Child: So, words always bring a reaction?

Spirit: Of course, words should encourage others rather than not.

Child: How can I do that?

Spirit: Listen.

Child: Listen to what?

Spirit: Not what, who.

Child: Then who?

Spirit: Another's message of words.

Child: Message of words?

Spirit: Words of power either convey assurance or fear. You and others have the choice of either, what would you choose?

Child: I would choose assurance.

Spirit: Yes, whether to console, give wisdom, bring happiness, and knowledge.

Child: Why do others say mean words?

Spirit: Power.

Child: Do you have to be mean to have power?

Spirit: No.

Child: What is power?

Spirit: Humankind knows power to be a form of control over someone or something.

Child: Well is it?

Spirit: No, power is about change in the form of growth hopefully for the better than worse.

Child: So, power is about change?

Spirit: Yes, and growth.

Child: I think I am beginning to understand.

Elder: Yes, I believe you are.

"To know courage is to have faith in yourself, hope in others, and love for another."

Colleen C. Carson

Path
Of
Courage

Child: Sorry, I was in my thoughts.

Elder: Yes, I know.

Child: Were you speaking to me about something?

Elder: No, I was in thought as well.

Child: I was wondering about something?

Elder: What is it your wondering about my child?

Child: What about hate?

Elder: What do you wish to know?

Child: Why do others hate?

Elder: The reason has been discussed.

Child: Why can't I remember?

Elder: You will.

Child: When?

Elder: When you are ready.

Child: Is hate powerful?

Elder: Only love has power.

Child: Do you mean hate has no power?

Elder: Only if you give hate power.

Child: Can I stop the hate?

Elder: Yes.

Child: How?

Elder: You. Live your tiger spirit within.

Child: I know I must respect others.

Elder: Yes, but even more importantly yourself.

Child: Why myself?

Elder: To respect others, you must respect yourself.

Child: If I respect others will I be successful?

Elder: Why are you concerned about success?

Child: I have been told and have seen what people look like that are not successful and I do not want to be them.

Elder: Who are these people?

Child: The poor.

Elder: What does the poor look like?

Child: They look sad.

Elder: Do you determine the poor by an emotion?

Child: No, they do not have anything.

Elder: What do you consider anything?

Child: House, clothes, money, and things.

Elder: You must not judge anyone based on your choice of happiness.

Child: What do you mean?

Elder: You have determined they are sad because they do not have what you have.

Child: No, they look sad and I feel bad for them.

Elder: Why do you think only the poor are sad?

Child: I do not but they seem to be like that all the time.

Elder: I see you have based your judgment on ignorance.

Child: No, older people have also told me, are they wrong?

Elder: Why do you question in a right or wrong?

Child: Well, you are either right or your wrong?

Elder: Why?

Child: I do not know, that is what I have been told.

Elder: Again, the what not the who.

Child: Okay, then what else is there other than right or wrong?

Elder: Life has many choices each offering a point of knowledge whether of disappointment or achievement in the knowing about you and the values from within. Your choice is simply a different lesson which is nor right or wrong.

Child: Are you saying I should not judge others?

Elder: That is a question only you can answer.

Child: What else but judgement?

Elder: Judgement is easy, how have you helped the sadden?

Child: I have not, but I can help them if I know how?

Elder: Take the time to learn before judging others.

Child: Do they need my help?

Elder: Yes, we are all here to help each other.

Child: How do you mean?

Elder: In your times of suffering, disappointment, needs or wants someone will be there to help you. Judgement is only motivated by ignorance.

Child: I do not want to be like that.

Elder: Remember; self-judgement or judgement of others will only bring you fear and even resentment.

Child: I am sorry, I did not mean to judge.

Elder: Lesson learned.

Child: I want to be successful.

Elder: The decision is yours.

Child: Do you think I can?

Elder: Does it truly matter what I think, when really, it is who you are?

Child: It matters to me.

Elder: What is your vision of achievement?

Child: I have always seen success as money.

Elder: Money has nothing to do with achievement.

Child: I do not understand?

Elder: Money is a need; achieving is a want.

Child: I have heard others say when you have lots of money you are successful, are they wrong?

Elder: They have been misled.

Child: How can you live without money?

Elder: We were not speaking of survival; we were speaking of achievement.

Child: What is the most successful goal in life?

Elder: You do not know?

Child: That is why I am asking you?

Elder: Love someone.

Child: Love is the most successful goal?

Elder: Of course.

Child: Do you mean there are no other successes?

Elder: I did not say that; you must listen child.

Child: How do you mean?

Elder: Achievement comes in many forms.

Child: What type of forms?

Elder: We have spoken about some of those forms regarding gifts. In time you will discover many in your journey of life lessons.

Child: So, love is the most successful goal.

Elder: Yes, also the most rewarding.

Child: Is love part of life lessons?

Elder: Yes.

Child: What is a life lesson again?

Elder: An experience which will teach you the student while a teacher in the student of thought.

Child: Is this what you meant by teacher and student?

Elder: Yes, your journey, your life story.

Child: Are you saying I will have my own life story?

Elder: Yes, we all have a story to tell.

Child: When do I start my story?

Elder: You already have.

Child: When did I start my story?

Elder: At first breath.

Child: Am I supposed to tell my story to others?

Elder: The choice is yours; we are all the storyteller of our life.

Child: I hope I can do this right.

Elder: How do you want the end of your story to be?

Child: An ending that will bring me and others joy.

Elder: Then treat each day as a love one you will never see again.

Child: That kind of sounds sad.

Elder: Remember; believe in you and your choices will come easier, and always be the influence of your own purpose. Choose to be the admirer of you and less the critic.

Child: What is a critic?

Elder: One who evaluates.

Child: What does evaluate mean?

Elder: It can be a review or judgement.

Child: I thought you said not to judge?

Elder: Judgement will only come with the obligation of perfection.

Child: But you said nothing is perfect other than your soul.

Elder: Yes, although humankind lives in the belief of the existence of perfection.

Child: I am beginning to realize that perfection is not a good thing.

Elder: I told you before; Life is a sequence of what you describe as failures and successes. There is a learnt wisdom from disappointment as equal to the bliss of achievement. To have balance in your life and know joy you must experience both. Humankind finds it easier to accept achieving rather than that of disappointment, which is unfortunate but understood.

Child: I am still not quite clear on why we must fail?

Elder: Disappointment is a pathway in the inspiration of chance and the accomplishment of wisdom.

Child: You still did not answer my question about hate?

Elder: I believe I did.

Child: Can you tell me again, please?

Elder: Hate has no power unless you give it power. Hate originates from the fear of the ignorant with the influence of cruelty.

Child: Can you see hate?

Elder: Yes. They who live in hate have a darkness within, which plagues their soul, they treat the truth with contempt and lies with honour. They are the broken ones.

Child: They are broken, how sad. Can they be helped?

Elder: Sometimes, but not always.

Child: I thought you said that everyone's soul is pure?
Elder: Yes. I also said you are given the choice to choose.

Child: Hate is horrible and sad.

Elder: Yes. Hate does not exist unless given power unlike love which exists on endless power.

Child: I must ask you something that confuses me?

Elder: Yes.

Child: I have heard others say nice things, but then change to saying mean things, and they are older than me. Why don't they know wisdom?

Elder: Yes, my child, I know them as well. They are the others who settled in the lack of knowledge while influenced by the ignorance of their contempt.

Child: How is it influenced?

Elder: You must listen child, as I told you by fear.

Child: Why are they like that?

Elder: They no longer seek the value in learning.

Child: I do not understand?

Elder: They stopped learning, teaching, refuse to follow and only wish to lead.

Child: What about their gifts of uniqueness?

Elder: They have banished their gifts into the realm of ignorance while living in their shadows of darkness.

Child: Can you help them remember their gifts?

Elder: They do not wish my aid they only want to profess my name.

Child: Why?

Elder: Control.

Child: What about their tiger spirit within?

Elder: They did not want to roar into the acceptance of diversity of truth.

Child: You say my tiger spirit is within, where?

Elder: Your soul, my child.

Child: You said our soul is about truth?

Elder: Yes.

Child: Only our soul is perfect?

Elder: Yes.

Child: What about our heart?

Elder: You already know about your heart.

Child: I do not understand?

Elder: Yes, you do.

Child: Please explain?

Elder: Your heart is love; your soul is truth.

Child: I still do not think I understand?

Elder: Your heart knows love.

Child: So, I know my heart through love?

Elder: Yes, when knowing love, you cherish your heart.

Child: I want to be a better person.

Elder: Yes.

Child: Did I tell you my name?

Elder: I know your name

Child: You do, what is my name?

Elder: Chance.

Child: How did you know my name?

Elder: We have met before.

Child: When, I cannot remember?

Elder: I do.

Child: What is your name?

Elder: Wisdom.

Child: Your name suits you, does mine suit me?

Elder: Yes, it does.

Child: I respect you, Wisdom.

Elder: I respect you, Chance.

Child: You do?

Elder: Yes.

Child: Why?

Elder: Because of the who of you.

Child: Really?

Elder: Yes.

Child: Will I see you again?

Elder: Yes.

Child: Are you sure?

Elder: Yes.

Child: Why are you sure?

Elder: It is our journey.

Child: Our journey?

Elder: Yes.

Child: Journey to where?

Elder: Truth.

Child: Truth in what?

Elder: Not what, who.

Child: You mean truth in others?

Elder: You and others.

Child: Is truth in Wisdom?

Elder: Yes.

Child: Will you get over your disappointment?

Elder: Perhaps.

Child: When?

Elder: When humankind's tiger spirit roars into the masses and empowers harmony amongst the beauty of each and all.

Child: Do you think that will happen?

Elder: I can only believe in the possibility.

Child: I have learned so much as your student and you my teacher.

Elder: No, my child that is not how one learns.

Child: Why do you say no?

Elder: Teacher and student are one.

Child: Again, I do not understand?

Elder: You will.

Child: Please let me understand?

Elder: Teacher and student; teach and learn at the same time.

Child: What have you learned from me?

Elder: The journey of innocence and opportunity.

Child: Really, what do you mean by innocence?

Elder: Your willingness in the want and need to know of others, the world you live in, and yourself in the opportunity of knowledge.

Child: I am going to have to go soon.

Elder: Yes.

Child: Another question?

Elder: Yes, my child, what is your question?

Child: Why do you tell me to listen so many times?

Elder: In order for you to understand the importance of listening.

Child: What is so important about listening?

Elder: Viewing the world through another's thoughts.

Child: Why would I need to do that?

Elder: I would hope you would want to.

Child: Why?

Elder: There are many reasons why.

Child: What are the reasons?

Elder: Respect in what others are saying has equal importance to your spoken words. Awareness in the who of another's knowledge in the diversity of humankind. Reason for another to share in the existence of your uniqueness.

Child: Listening is important?

Elder: Yes, listening will always create an innovative chance in the mastering of wisdom.

Child: I will learn to listen better.

Elder: Well-chosen.

Child: I live in Destiny do you know where it is?

Elder: I know it well.

Child: Where do you live Wisdom?

Elder: I live in Joy.

Child: Would I be able to find Joy?

Elder: Yes.

Child: How do I get there?

Elder: You must travel the path of courage.

Child: Have you travelled the path of courage?

Elder: Yes, numerous times.

Child: What is it like?

Elder: It is challenging.

Child: Challenging, why?

Elder: You will see.

Child: Should I be frightened?

Elder: No.

Child: Do I have to be brave?

Elder: Yes.

Child: I do not know if I can.

Elder: Who is your courage?

Child: I guess, my dad and mom?

Elder: You see their courage. Who is your courage?

Child: Me?

Elder: Yes. The path of courage is only for the courageous.

Child: I am still kind of scare?

Elder: Do not be.

Child: Will I be alone?

Elder: No, there will be many.

Child: Will I meet anyone of these many?

Elder: Yes.

Child: Who?

Elder: The first will greet you at the beginning of the path.

Child: What is his name?

Elder: She goes by the name of Faith.

Child: How will I recognize Faith?

Elder: She will be the confidence in the trusting of your courage; the who of you.

Child: Please explain, I am not sure I understand?

Elder: The assurance that the things revealed and promised are true, even though unseen, and gives you belief and confidence.

Child: How will I know her, I do not know what she looks like?

Elder: She will welcome you.

Child: Why?

Elder: Once you meet, you will know your answer.

Child: Will Faith walk the whole path of courage with me.

Elder: That will be your choice.

Child: Will I meet anyone else?

Elder: Yes.

Child: Who will he be?

Elder: Her name is Hope.

Child: What does she look like?

Elder: Faith knows her.

Child: Will I like her?

Elder: Yes, very much so.

Child: What part of the path will we meet?

Elder: That depends on you.

Child: How will I recognize Hope?

Elder: She will be the certainty in the aspiration of your courage; the what of you.

Child: Will Hope walk with Faith and me?

Elder: Again, that will be your choice.

Child: I have got a feeling I will like both Faith and Hope.

Elder: Yes.

Child: Will I meet anyone else?

Elder: There will be one other.

Child: When will I meet her?

Elder: When you are ready.

Child: When I am ready?

Elder: Yes.

Child: I am confused?

Elder: Yes.

Child: With Faith and Hope I will meet them through the path, but with the third one I decide whether I will or not, why?

Elder: Life choices.

Child: I do not understand?

Elder: Others will choose to meet you and you will choose to meet others.

Child: What is this person's name?

Elder: Her name is Charity, but many call her Love.

Child: Why two names?

Elder: Ask Charity she will be happy to tell you.

Child: How will I recognize Love or Charity?

Elder: She will be the credibility in the promise of your courage; the why of you.

Child: I think I am going to call her Love.

Elder: The choice is yours.

Child: I noticed my courage seems to have a lot to do with confidence?

Elder: Yes, you cannot have courage without a sense of confidence.

Child: So, then I will not be alone?

Elder: I told you no one is alone.

Child: Oh yes, you did tell me that.

Elder: Yes.

Child: So, you know Faith, Hope, and Love?

Elder: Yes.

Child: How long have you known them?

Elder: Infinity.

Child: How long is infinity?

Elder: It is a very long time.

Child: Why will they be on this path?

Elder: I believe I told you.

Child: Can you just tell me again?

Elder: Purpose of certainty, confidence, and credibility.

Child: I think I now understand; can I explain?

Elder: I believe you do, I am listening.

Child: You said the path of courage is challenging, I will have to be brave. I believe to appreciate my purpose I must have courage to seek it.

Elder: Yes.

Child: That knowledge is important because without it I will live in ignorance and fear causing me not to achieve my purpose.

Elder: Very well said.

Child: I also believe that to live my purpose in my destiny I must journey with hope, faith, and love to achieve joy.

Elder: I am proud of you.

Child: You know what Wisdom; I think I am proud of me too?

Elder: Yes, I believe you are.

Child: Do you want me to say hi to them for you?

Elder: Yes, that would be truly kind of you.

Child: Why don't I feel frightened as I did?

Elder: Knowledge.

Child: Yes, knowledge of the who, what and why of me and others.

Elder: You better go now.

Child: Wisdom I know you will be in my thoughts.

Elder: Yes, Chance, I will.

Child: Will I be able to see you here, again?

Elder: I will seek you.

Child: I cannot seek you?

Elder: You won't have too.

Child: Why?

Elder: I will forever be in your thoughts.

Child: Wisdom, I know I will not be bullied again.

Elder: Why Chance?

Child: Trust me, you will hear my roar, just listen for it.

Elder: I will be there.

Child: Good day.

Elder: Hello

TIGER SPIRIT WITHIN

WHO

WHAT

WHY

will allow the chance of
opportunities to discover
your purpose and the
wisdom of courage.

Colleen C. Carson

TIGER SPIRIT WITHIN

"Family is like branches on a tree, we all grow in different directions, yet our roots remain as one."

Unknown

"We all live in the forest of life where there is no tree that stands alone."

Colleen C. Carson

TIGER SPIRIT WITHIN

FACTS

Children's Schoolyard

1. Suicide is the third leading cause of death among young people. (A study in Britain found that at least half of suicides among young people are related to bullying.)

2. Bully victims are between 2 to 9 times more likely to consider suicide than non-victims. (Yale University)

3. Approximately 160,000 teens skip school every day because of bullying. (NEA)

4. 1 in 4 teachers see nothing wrong with bullying and will only intervene 4% of the time. (NASP)

5. 282,000 students are physically attacked in secondary schools each month. (Gov.ca)

6. 9 out of 10 LGBTQ students experienced harassment at school and online. (Bullying Statistics)

7. 1 in 5 Canadian Teens has witnessed online Bullying. (UBC)

8. At least 1 in 3 adolescent students in Canada have reported being bullied recently. (Gov.ca)

9. 17% of American students report being bullied 2 to 3 times a month or more within a school semester. (NASP)

Corporate Schoolyard

1. Every target of a bully may lose up to 200 working hours of productivity annually. (Stomp Out Bullying)

2. Workplace bullying is on the rise half of all workers have been affected by workplace bullying. (WBI)

3. 1 in 3 people face some sort of bullying in the workplace (Workplace Bullying Institute)

4. 40% of Canadian workers experience bullying on a weekly basis (Gov.ca)

5. 75% of employees surveyed had been affected by workplace bullying, whether as a target or a witness. (University of Phoenix)

6. Negative comments due to race or ethnicity were experienced by 7.4% of respondents, while unfair treatment due to gender was experienced by 10.9%. (HCA)

7. 52% of women have experienced bullying or harassment at work in the past three years. (Opportunity Now)

8. There is a culture of silence around bullying, with only 1% of people saying they had reported it. Workplace culture encourages people to leave rather than report problems. (Opportunity Now)

9. Race plays a large role in workplace bullying. (Wikipedia)

The Global Schoolyard of Politicians, Leaders, and Representatives

1. Use words, statements, and name-calling to gain power and control.

2. Talking badly about their opponents and others that are not on their team.

3. Making fun of others for who they are, how they dress or look.

4. Messaging malicious rumors on social media.

5. Shaming or intimidating opponents online.

6. Use pressure to get colleagues or partisans to participate in their bullying.

7. Blame-shifting a form of deflection taking the attention away from themselves.

8. For personal gain or profit sabotaging someone's reputation.

9. It is a mode of lying and distortion against rival candidates.

10. Bullying voters to prevent them from casting their vote.

WHAT KIDS NEED TO KNOW:

- Never give out personal information online.

- Never give out your password to anyone other than your parents.
- If someone sends you a horrible message show it immediately to a parent or adult.

- Do not open emails from strangers or bullies.

- Do not put anything online or in an email that you do not want the world to see.
- Do not send angry (negative) emails because you will receive one back.

- Treat others as you would like to be treated.

- Teach your parents about cyber-bullying, together you can prevent it.

- Tell an adult if you see someone being bullied or if you are being bullied.

- Remember a bully lacks confidence.

WHAT PARENTS CAN DO:

- Discuss bullying and cyber-bullying with your children as soon as you know they can understand which should be around three years old.

- Discuss being bullied and being the bully do not think your child is not capable of being a bully.

- Keep your home computer in a busy area of your house and check on what they are doing every so often.

- Do not allow your children to give out any personal information.

- Know your children's screen names and passwords.

- Regularly go over their list of their online connections with them.

- Ask about each person is (connection) and how your children know him or her.

- Discuss bullying and cyber-bullying with your children.
- Ask them if they have ever experienced it or seen it happen to someone.

- Emphasize that you will not blame your children if they are cyber-bullied, nor take away their computer privileges.

- If you can always get involved in your children's school and activities and keep communication open .
- Watch for any aggressive behaviour or signs of depression.

- Eating habits might change.

- Not wanting to go to school or to their activities.

- Anti-Bullying Hotlines in the US and Canada; Listed below are several hotlines serving youth in Canada and the USA that you can call when you need to talk. Please Google there are more throughout these countries and internationally.

1-800-668-6868
Canada Kids Help Phone

1-800-399-PEER
Peer listening line for those under 25 years old.

1-800-SUICIDE or 1-800-273-TALK (8255)

1-800-442-HOPE
National Youth Crisis Hotline for crisis intervention and school tip line for reporting weapons or homicidal remarks.

1-800-999-9999
Covenant House NineLine dealing with crisis intervention and angry feelings.

1-800-784-2433

National Hopeline connects caller to a 24-hour crisis center in their area.

ORGANIZATIONS

Dove Self-Esteem Project	www.dove.com
Kidpower	www.kidpower.org
Born This Way Foundation	www.bornthisway.foundation
Stomp Out Bullying	www.stompoutbullying.org
Kind Campaign	www.kindcampaign.com
Dare To Care	www.daretocare.ca
Pacer Center	www.pacer.org
Free 2 Luv	www.free2luv.org
Canadian Red Cross	www.redcross.ca
Erase Bullying	www.erasebullying.ca

Colleen's Other Books:

- The Guyed Book - Self-help on how-to romance a Woman Love and Romance

- A Fare Chance Cookbook – He will & She will Keep It Savoir Simple

theguyedbook.com

Colleen's Songs:
- You Do not Touch Me Like You Do (About Relationship)
- We Revolution (About Mother Earth)
- We Rise (About Bullying)
- My Shattered Heart (About Loss of a Child)
- I Promise (coming soon) (About Love)

"Always say, I love you to your love ones as if there's no tomorrow."

Colleen C. Carson

Manufactured by Amazon.ca
Bolton, ON